PARIS

PARIS

SANDRA FORTY

GRAMERCY BOOKS
NEW YORK

This 2000 edition is published by Gramercy Books™,
a division of Random House Value Publishing, Inc.,
280 Park Avenue, New York, NY 10017.
by arrangement with PRC Publishing Ltd, London.

Gramercy Books™ and design are registered trademarks of
Random House Value Publishing, Inc.
Random House
New York • Toronto • London • Sydney • Auckland
http://www.randomhouse.com/

Printed and bound in China
A CIP catalogue record for this book is available from the Library of Congress.

ISBN 0-517-16175-3

8 7 6 5 4 3 2 1

ACKNOWLEDGEMENTS

The publisher wishes to thank Pictor International - London for supplying all the photography for this book,
including the photographs on the front and back covers, with the following exceptions:

Stewart Kendall/Allstar for pages 18, 47 and 116; Duncan Willetts/Allstar for pages 23, 54, 90 and 91;
© Robert Holmes/CORBIS for pages 26, 42-43, 56-57, 62, 63, 70-71, 74-75, 102-103, 124, 126 and 127;
© Harald A Jahn; Viennaslide Photoagency/CORBIS for pages 36-37; © Paul Almasy/CORBIS for page 39;
David Davies/Allstar for pages 48, 52, 59 and 120; © The Purcell Team/CORBIS for pages 60-61;
© Leonard de Selva/CORBIS for pages 64-65; © ART on FILE/CORBIS for pages 82-83;
© Stefano Bianchetti/CORBIS for pages 86-87 and 122-123; © A.N.T. Photo-Library for page 94;
© Bill Ross/CORBIS for pages 96-97; © Owen Franken/CORBIS for pages 100-101;
© Stephanie Colasanti/CORBIS for page 117; © Catherine Karnow/CORBIS for page 121.

Previous page:
Arc de Triomphe
Twelve avenues meet at Étoile where the largest and most famous triumphal arch in the world
still dominates its surroundings. It was dedicated to the glory of Napoleon's Grand Army
and built in two stages, 1806–14, then finished in 1836.

Cover:
Eiffel Tower
Does anything sum up Paris better than the tower? Elegant, stately, and immediately recognizable.

CONTENTS

INTRODUCTION

Paris is not the obvious geographical location for the capital of France—it is too far north and west—yet all the country's major roads and transport links converge on Paris, and France is one of the most centralized countries in the world. There are many reasons why Paris became the capital, but ultimately it was the choice of French monarchs to live in or near the city and their stranglehold on French politics that enforced Parisian ascendancy.

Paris is a modern thriving city, undoubtedly one of the greatest and most beautiful in the world, but alongside that accolade, Paris has all the problems of a modern city—pollution, overcrowding, congested traffic. These may appear to be modern dilemmas, but Paris has suffered from all them to a greater or lesser extent for most of its history. As the well-established center of France—the center of political, administrative and cultural life—the capital has traditionally attracted people from outlying districts as well as the provinces to search for jobs and a better lifestyle: it always has been over-crowded. In turn, too many people and difficulties in procuring fresh water has exacerbated pollution problems.

Paris is a city of great contrasts, with the old sitting right next to the ultra-modern. Unlike many other European cities, Paris has not suffered much from enemy action despite being in disputed territory for both of the world wars. In fact Paris only sustained about 8% destruction during World War II in spite of being occupied by the Nazis for four years. The last major destruction of Paris by any but her own citizens was by the Vikings way back in the 9th century. Furthermore, even in the days when the buildings were built primarily from wood, there was no fire of any consequence which substantially altered the face of the city.

Most of the damage that has been done to Paris has been perpetrated by Frenchmen—during the civil war between the Communards and the State in 1871, and later through the efforts of Emperor Napoleon III and Haussmann when entire swathes of the city were razed to create the grand boulevards and avenues which still dominate the center of Paris. Another grand plan, luckily never adopted, was proposed by the French architect Le Corbusier in 1925. He wanted to flatten much of the center of Paris and build instead eighteen

Left:

La Défense

Now the prosperous business center of Paris, this area was named after a monument commemorating the defense of Paris in 1871 during the Franco-Prussian War.

identical giant towers right in the heart of the city! As in other countries, however, there has been civic vandalism in the name of modernization, perhaps the most notable of which was the destruction of the old trading area of Les Halles with its magnificent glass and iron market halls to make way for an indifferent shopping mall. A fragment of the building remains as an indication of the magnificence of the lost buildings.

The History of Paris

Paris sits in the middle of the great flood plain basin of the River Seine and its tributaries. The area was already settled in prehistoric times and even then was at the crossroads of trading routes between the northern Europe (now Germany) and Spain and the Mediterranean. The area, as well as being treacherously marshy, flooded frequently: the only secure dry ground was a largish island in the middle of the river. Whoever possessed the island controlled the area, and this island—later called the Île de la Cité—proved crucial to the successful establishment of Paris.

By 250 BC the island was inhabited by a Gallic tribe of copper-working boatmen, fishermen, foresters, and herdsmen. They called their settlement "Lutetia" from the Latin for marsh. Later, the island was invaded and settled by the Quarisii Celts (who later became the Parisii). They brought iron with them, and had the skills and initiative to build two wooden bridges across to La Cité. They charged a toll to cross these bridges and made themselves wealthy on the proceeds. They were a clever people, particularly good at trading, and grew prosperous as the river crossing saved traders a huge detour around the Seine and made Lutetia the principal crossroads of northern Gaul.

The greatest threat to the Parisii came from the encroaching Roman legions. Rightly worried, the Parisii sent 8,000 men to the Celt leader Vercingetorix, who led a revolt of tribes against Rome, to help him fight the invaders; this proved futile as Vercingetorix and his warriors were beaten and all but wiped out at Alesia in 52 BC. Vercingetorix himself was captured and taken to Rome. The Romans, always appreciative of strategic importance and impressed by income potential, turned their attention to Lutetia.

Of such importance was this site, 90 miles (145km) from the Channel, that its first written mention was made by Julius Caesar in his book on the Gallic Wars when he talked of the city of the Parisii on an island in the Seine. With the legion marching on their domain, the Parisii retreated to La Cité, burning their fortress and cult sites as well as their two precious bridges behind them. This only held off the Romans for a short time. With Roman organization and drive, La Cité became even more prosperous and a concerted building program started on the island itself and on the higher ground to the south.

Trade came to Lutetia mostly by river, and it was also probably a big agricultural market place for local produce. The Romans did not make it their headquarters in Gaul—that honor went instead to Reims. However, they did build they city around them to their standards and expectations—a city wall, a forum, a temple, three baths (there are still remains at Cluny), and a 10,000-seat arena (Arènes de Lutèce), of which there are also some remains to be seen. A number of statues and monuments were erected, and as the city grew, the swamps that hampered development were drained and filled in. It has been estimated that, at its height, Roman Lutetia numbered around 10,000 people and covered about 370 acres.

Around AD 250 an Athenian preacher, Denis, was sent to Lutetia to convert the pagans. He became the first bishop of Lutetia and its first saint. The story goes that, with two accomplices, he set about destroying the pagan statues. They were all arrested, and had their heads chopped off on Mons Mortis (Mount Mercury), now Montmartre. However, by the time of his death Denis had apparently achieved his aim of Christianizing the populace.

By the middle of the 4th century AD Lutetia had became known as Paris—named after the original Celtic Parisii—and was a prosperous city. But within fifty years, by the end of the century, Rome was retreating in the face of invading and rampaging Barbarian hordes; Gaul in particular was susceptible and the invaders raided the upper reaches of Lutetia but were unable to fight their way across to the island. It was decided to abandon the Left Bank and everyone moved to the safety of the island. Hampered by the lack of resources, the Romans did the only thing they could and demolished many of their formal buildings to provide stone for the first town wall. However, it did not stem the tide elsewhere, and soon the threat to Rome herself became paramount, and the Romans abandoned their possessions in northern Gaul.

Tradition has it that in AD 451 Attila the Hun bore down on Paris with evil intent. The population prepared to flee, but was saved by Ste. Geneviève. She spoke to the people and convinced them they would be safe if they repented their sins and prayed for forgiveness. Most of them must have done so because, incredibly, Attila ignored Paris to raid southward—St. Geneviève was praised as the savior of Paris.

In 486 Paris was finally conquered—by the Franks, but much later than the rest of Gaul, testimony to the defensive qualities of Île de la Cité as well as the Roman legacy of organization and fighting ability. Clovis, who was in all probability the leader of the Franks, chose to base himself in Paris (in 508) and make it the center of his kingdom, from where he could oversee his newly conquered southern territories. Furthermore, to reinforce his position he determined to make Paris an orthodox Christian center instead of the rival Tours. Consequently, the foundation of many churches and abbeys date from around this time.

His grandson, Clovis I (481-511), founder of the Merovingian dynasty, made Paris his official capital, a status the city has enjoyed almost continuously ever since. Within 100 years Paris had established its political supremacy over its principal rivals—Soissons, Orléans, Reims, Tours and, in particular, over near-by St.-Denis, which had a palace, the royal burial grounds and, most importantly, the mint.

The population of Paris was growing and the overspill tended to congregate around the great monasteries on both sides of the Seine. By about AD 700 Paris and St.-Denis started to join up, linked by the St.-Denis fairground. Between the 6th and the 10th centuries AD the marshes on the Right Bank and the drier plains on the Left Bank gradually became church property, and villages started to grow around the protected area of the larger foundations. Urban sprawl had started.

Paris suffered a setback during the Carolingian dynasty (768–814) when the emperor Charlemagne turned his back on the city in favor of Aix-la-Chapelle (Aachen), from where he could rule Germany and Italy as well. But his empire gradually disintegrated after his death through the equal division of territory between his sons and their heirs.

Despite losing her political position, Paris was still an important crossroads and trading center. By this time there were around 20–30,000 inhabitants — a sizable city for those times. All this made Paris too enticing for the Vikings, who attacked and pillaged the surrounding area in 885–86, but even then they could not get to La Cité. In fury they wreaked vengeance on the south bank, reducing the buildings to rubble and returning the land to agriculture. Thwarted, the Vikings made their main base further south, around Rouen about 85 miles away, and settled what became the Duchy of Normandy. The need to harness their greedy aggression would ultimately ensure the strategic importance of Paris.

The founder of the Capetian dynasty (987–1328) was Hugh Capet, chosen by his peers at Senlis in 987. He made his residence the palace on the Île de la Cité and assumed many of the trappings of kingship. This action would, in the long term, establish the pre-eminence of Paris even though at the time Champagne was more important commercially and internationally, and Laon and Chartres held the great schools of learning. The Capetian dynasty worked hard to emphasize its own importance and that of its capital, to make Paris the base to unite a divided country, a task made easier by the always menacing Anglo-Norman threat.

At the turn of the 12th century the structure of Paris was starting to emerge; still an agricultural town there were large areas of cultivated ground enclosed and protected by walls — thirty on the Left Bank and twelve on the right. Most commerce and all the prosperity were due to the Seine — Paris earned a rich living from imposing taxes and duties on all goods transported

Right:
Eiffel Tower
Built as the temporary centerpiece of the 1889 Paris Exposition, the Eiffel Tower commemorates the centenary of the French Revolution.

by water. Politically, too, the town was taking shape: one of the king's officers was made Provost of Paris, the governor of the town and chief of police.

It was under Philippe Auguste (1180–1223) that Paris really blossomed. The Anglo-Norman presence only forty miles away gave Paris an unrivaled strategic importance; furthermore, Philippe Auguste was determined to make his chosen seat of government the financial, commercial, and intellectual heart of France. To do this he embarked on a huge program of building and development. More of the surrounding marshes were drained to allow more grain to be grown; access across the Seine was improved by the building of more bridges; the two ancient wooden ones were rebuilt with fortifications (châtelets) and a number of the muddy streets of the Cité were paved.

New buildings altered the skyline, including the start of Notre-Dame and the Temple; two enclosed markets were built at Champeaux, and the Innocents graveyard was enclosed. In addition a great many private homes were built. Pope Innocent III granted statutes to create the first University on the Left Bank out of the existing schools in Paris.

Trade was still paramount for economic survival, and about this time the Hanse Parisienne was set up by the merchants of Paris, the significance being that this marked the foundation of the municipality. Their main economic rivals were to the north in Rouen, which had the advantage of being further down the Seine and closer to the Channel. Administratively Paris was organized into four districts—the French love of order was emerging.

The biggest scheme was the fortification of Paris itself. Philippe Auguste ordered the building of 3.3 miles of walls to encompass more than 620 acres, all dominated by the massive fortress of the Louvre. Although the walls were built to leave plenty of room for expansion, the space was rapidly occupied by the influx of workers needed to build and supply the many building projects. As ever, wherever there are people there is a problem of human waste—a constant thorn in the side of the city fathers—the first proper sewer, the Fossés-le-Roi, was cut through the swamp in 1260 to remove sewerage.

By 1240 Paris had grown to such an extent that the king, Louis VIII, had no option but to grant permission to build outside the city walls. Paris was now indisputably the capital of France. The great theological Collège de Sorbonne was founded and attracted great eminences like St. Thomas Aquinas. The custom of appealing to the king for justice had been established by Philippe Auguste, and the monarch's prestige had made Paris the center of European diplomatic activity. The provost's office was reorganized in 1261 and divided between the provost of the king, who dealt with affairs of state, and the provost of the merchants, whose business was to oversee local affairs.

Successive French kings reinforced this centralization of Paris and the influence of her merchants, judiciary, politicians, and culture. In particular, financial institutions and the judiciary expanded. Fiscal records imply that Paris was the third largest city in Europe (after Venice and Milan) with a population of about 80,000, and about twice the size of London. However, the people were crammed in at a density of seventy-four per acre which was in all likelihood the highest in Europe. The density was highest in the poorer Left Bank and La Cité areas, and much less so in the wealthy Right Bank districts of Grève and St.-Germain-l'Auxerrois. The road network across France, which had converged on Lyons around this time, shifted to focus on Paris, and so it has remained ever since.

For young Frenchmen wanting to make their fortune Paris was a magnet, and around the 1350s the city was rapidly expanding to accommodate the influx. Builders were employed creating new streets of homes for the middle classes, as well as houses for the wealthy on the outskirts near the Louvre, in the Marais and Mont Ste.-Geneviève. Increasing numbers of foreigners came to Paris as the influence of the University as the pre-eminent seat of learning in Europe spread and Paris's importance as a center of international finance and diplomacy increased.

In 1328 the House of Valois (1328–1589) ascended to the French throne with Philippe VI (1328-50). But nine years later the costly Hundred Years' War against England started, and a few years later, in mid-century, the devastating Black Death arrived. Bubonic plague figures have not survived for Paris, but elsewhere in France the population halved, so it can be reasonably supposed that with the population density and general insanitary living conditions in Paris, the effects there were even worse. Just after, in 1355 the people of Paris first declared themselves an independent commune under the leadership of Étienne Marcel. This lasted for three years.

Because of the war, a new city wall was started in 1356 on the Right Bank by the provost of merchants. This was continued and finished by Charles V (1364–80); the resulting wall was 26–33ft high and encompassed 430 acres outside the previous wall. At intervals along it were six small fortresses (bastilles) and the entire structure was encircled by a double moat. Meanwhile the wall on the Left Bank, built by Philippe Auguste, was modernized and reinforced. Paris now covered some 1,084 enclosed acres. The massive fortress of the Bastille itself was built, with eight tall towers, and the Louvre was yet again restored, enlarged, and improved. All this work put pressure on the economy, leading to rises in taxes to pay for the building as well as the continuing Hundred Years' War. Charles V became increasingly unpopular and when rioters threatened his life, he moved his residence to the Hôtel St.-Paul near the protection of his new Bastille. Even this was too exposed and he decided to move outside Paris altogether: the Château at Vincennes was chosen and fortified. From then on the monarch lived outside Paris as his security could only be guaranteed for short periods in the city. On Charles V's death the population rioted again against the ever-increasing tax burden.

By natural progression Paris had divided itself into three districts—to the north around the Place de Grève (now Place de l'Hôtel de Ville) lived all the merchants; in the middle on the Île de la Cité were all the administrative offices for Paris and France as a whole; and on the Left Bank the spiritual and intellectual life centered on the university in the Latin Quarter. Life for the poor was still indescribably squalid and hard: rents and taxes kept going up and times were hard. As ever with money the blame was deflected onto the Jews, and they were expelled from Paris in 1394.

During the reign of Charles VII (1422–61) the perennial problems of lack of living space, foul water, and dreadful sanitation combined with high rents and taxation brought many to the brink of starvation and insurrection. The revolt of the Maillotins was the inevitable consequence, but they were mercilessly suppressed.

For a brief period in 1431 the English took control of Paris, causing the French heroine Jeanne d'Arc (1412–31) and her followers to besiege the city in vain. That same year Henry V of England had himself crowned king of France in Notre-Dame, but his claim was short-lived. Meanwhile, in the streets of Paris crime and rioting became common occurrences; all effective French government collapsed and a state of anarchy ensued.

After the retreat of the English and the ending of the war it took some 20 years for the economic recovery to take hold. Once again Paris attracted people from all over France, and by 1500 the city was back to full capacity, its prosperity in its financial institutions and the bourgeoisie who invested in commerce, particularly that of Marseille, Toulouse, and Rouen.

The financial and administrative structures of France started to change with the reign of Louis XI (1461–83). He ruthlessly set about changing the existing medieval institutions to a more streamlined and autocratic establishment. A major barrier to this endeavor were the great feudal lordships, especially the Burgundians and Normans, but they were pitilessly crushed by the king. In 1466 the Black Death struck again, devastating the populations of France and Paris.

The building of the Notre-Dame bridge between 1506–12 is generally seen as signalling Paris's return to prosperity, although the period saw constant war and the return of the plague. When François I came to the throne in 1515 Paris had reached its physical limit with the swamps to the east and north preventing further growth. By this time Paris was a tortuous maze of winding streets which hindered rather than helped the flow of traffic and trade. In addition the population—somewhere around 150,000–200,000—was far too numerous for the accommodation, leading to chronic overcrowding and insanitary living conditions. To compound matters, despite having a huge river flowing through the heart of the city, there was a critical lack of clean fresh water. The Left Bank did not even have a fountain to supply it. The very air in some districts was so foul smelling that they were avoided as much as possible. François was anxious to stop expansion into the suburbs because it made the city less easy to defend, and so he ordered the dumps cleared and moved to make way for building sites and even gave up a number of his residences to alleviate the problem. But the sheer population pressure pushed the suburbs out especially to the west. For the poor, housing was near impossible, and for those with rooms the rents went up constantly. By the mid-16th century a man could not rent a complete house on a modest salary.

Paris was in crisis: it was still a major investment and economic center although the activity had declined to the extent that Paris redistributed very few goods and exported nothing. Traffic in the city had become so congested and trade slowed to such an extent that in an attempt to ease the situation private carriages were banned altogether in 1563. All the elements for insurrection were ripe.

During the 16th century, Protestantism had arrived in Paris and religious unity became a major issue in France as in the rest of Europe. The first Protestants were executed in 1523, and as time progressed Paris became increasingly unsafe for followers of the new religion. Fanatical preachers openly stirred up the mob by urging for the massacre of all Protestants. On St. Bartholomew's Eve 1572, Catherine de Medici signed the order for the massacre of the Huguenot leaders in Paris and the mob took over: it is conservatively estimated that around 2,000 people were slaughtered and the streets of Paris were literally running with blood. The Religious Wars ripped France apart. In 1589 the Protestant king of Navarre (the future Henri IV) besieged Paris. Within a few months nearly 15,000 people died of famine. When Paris finally fell the city was declared guilt of felony and stripped of all rights and privileges which were then taken in hand by the crown. The War was largely ended by the signing of the Edict of Nantes in 1589.

After the long wars and siege Paris was in ruins, starving mobs terrorized the streets, and much of the suburbs had been razed. The king used his troops to suppress any insurrection, and then set about a public works program to revive the city. The palaces of the Louvre and Tuileries were refurbished and enlarged, the Pont Neuf was completed, and the Hôtel de Ville (town hall) started in 1594. To alleviate the problem of congested streets, in 1607 the king instigated the building line, making the alignment of buildings compulsory, and also prohibiting buildings of wooden construction and those with overhanging stories. To improve the streets themselves he ordered paving, and where possible widening.

Henri realized he had to sort out the problem of sanitation and attempted to imposed strict laws concerning waste disposal. As for the long-term problem of lack of fresh water, he had a hydraulically operated machine installed in the Seine. This was the famous Pont-Neuf pump (the Samaritaine) which relieved the situation slightly and provided running water for the Right Bank until 1813.

All this time, the suburbs of Paris expanded in line with the population. From the end of the wars of religion until 1640, Paris underwent one of its greatest periods of expansion. In 1590 the population was around 200,000, within forty years this figure had doubled.

In the 17th century Paris saw buildings and projects springing up everywhere. In 1616 the first gardens were laid out along the Cours de la Reine; popular from the start, they were extended and improved until they became known as the Champs-Élysées. Despite the building regulations of previous times, speculators developed town houses at will all over Paris. In forty years the price of land increased sixty times and rents shot up.

The Left Bank became fashionable when the Medici palace (Palais du Luxembourg) was built by Marie de Medici, and the Arcueil viaduct was constructed to bring much needed water to it and the district. Entire new quarters were established—Pré-aux-Clercs (Faubourg St.-Germain), and the Marais, which became the residential arrondissement for the aristocracy. Cardinal Richelieu built himself the Palais-Cardinal (now the Palais Royal). At this time also the Île des Vaches, an uninhabited island in the middle of the Seine, was linked by bridge to the Île de la Cité and renamed Île Saint-Louis. A fifth city wall was constructed in 1635. To reduce the danger of pestilence and vermin, as well as to provide new building land, the city dumps were cleared and removed to beyond the swamps; but the Seine was still being poisoned by all the raw sewage.

While all this commercial and private building was going on, the church was extending its holdings. Between 1600 and 1640 as many as sixty monasteries were founded in the Paris area. (By 1700 this figure had reached 110 monasteries in Paris alone.) To signify this great expansion, Paris became an archbishopric in 1622.

The bubble had to burst, and it did along with a general European economic slump between 1630 and 1640. The depression in France lasted much longer, roughly 1650–1730 and the growth of Paris slowed down almost to a halt. The Roi Soleil, Louis XIV (1643–1715) was so extravagant with his wars and luxurious court living that he all but bankrupted France. Economic depression meant that rents dropped, but Paris was swamped by the poor, especially rural peasants arriving in the capital hoping for work—it is calculated that 48,000 beggars thronged the streets. Greedy merchants ignored the ominous signs of unrest for short-term profit and poverty increased even among those who had a job. Yet again the situation was ripe for revolt and insurrection erupted in 1648 in the civil war known as the Fronde. The mob, as always, joined in enthusiastically.

Under Louis XIV, despite the depression, Paris again expanded its boundaries; in 1652 the city covered over 2,000 acres, and by 1715 it covered more than 2,750 acres. In 1670 Minister Colbert instigated an annual census of births, marriages, and deaths. From these it appears that the population of Paris reached around 500,000 in 1715. However, the figures reveal that the twin problems of overcrowding and lack of adequate sanitation made the mortality rate higher than the birth rate and any increase of population was down to rural migration. The situation defied all civic efforts although by 1670 there were fifteen fountains across the city bringing water to the people. One innovation was to light some of the streets at night with 6,500 candle-illuminated lanterns.

To glorify his reign, Louis XIV embarked upon a number of big projects under the direction of Colbert. The gardens of the Tuileries were set out, and the Invalides and Salpêtrière Hospital founded. As Louis triumphed abroad in his costly wars, he commemorated his victories with triumphal arches at the city gates, at Saint-Antoine, Saint-Martin and Saint-Denis. By the end of his reign Paris was the biggest city with the biggest population in Europe, and easily the most important economic center in France. In 1674 a securities' market was opened in Paris—the forerunner of the Bourse, the Paris stock exchange.

The expansion of Paris had the effect of making the city walls redundant and they were increasingly breached and the stone taken for new housing. Since Roman times Paris has been largely built of gypsum and limestone quarried from underground—to this day there are some 186 miles of underground tunnels under the Left Bank alone. The city itself was an increasingly convoluted maze of narrow streets and alleyways, only some 15ft wide, making the passage of traffic almost impossible. This was a major problem as it was already hard enough to bring sufficient food into the city to feed the population, let alone distribute it. Feeding Paris was such a task that the king gave his regional police lieutenants executive power to commandeer food for the city. Entire regions of France starved in times of poor harvest because all the produce was sent to Paris.

The court of Louis XIV was deemed responsible for bringing so many people to Paris, and in a vain attempt to stop the expansion of the city through illegal building, it was decided to move the court even further outside the city to Versailles—this move was effected after costly rebuilding and extensions in 1678. The court made huge demands on the royal purse strings and in turn on the French taxpayers. To satisfy the king's insatiable appetite for luxuries, thousands of workers came to Paris to work in the glass, silk, furniture, and tapestry industries. The Gobelin tapestry factory was founded for this purpose alone. When Louis XIV died in 1715 leaving France near-bankrupt many of these workers lost their jobs as their industries collapsed. When the Revolution came those who were left lost their jobs altogether as more industries collapsed overnight. To follow the king's example, and to escape the atrocious smell and congestion of the city, the wealthy and aristocracy bought country houses—many of them in the vicinity of Versailles.

Paris was the undisputed intellectual capital of Europe, with scholars from around Europe attracted by the university which had also become a scientific center, but the city was an unregulated sprawl. To exercise a measure of control and prevent new in-fill building, the numbering of houses started in the

Above:

Rue Mouffetard

Typical Parisian apartment buildings.

suburbs in 1728 (Paris itself did not follow suit until 1780); the following year street name signs appeared for the first time. In 1757, oil lamps illuminated Paris for the first time.

By the mid-18th century, Paris was again bursting at the seams. Futile attempts were again made to control the size of the city. Despite the crippling cost of wars and taxes, the swamps were drained more effectively and building spread out over the drying land. Entire districts of multi-storied buildings were built by the wealthy, who moved from area to area as fashion dictated. Most of the court nobility, when they weren't at Versailles, lived in St.-Germain; the bankers lived around Chausée d'Antin and Palais-Royal; while the legal profession occupied the new district of the Marais. Still the rich and influential flocked to Paris to be near the king and the centers of influence, depriving the provinces of their abilities and wealth.

The poor had no such luxury; those that did not live in the slums at the heart of Paris or in the stews of St.-Michel were forced to shift further and further out to avoid crippling rent increases. Time and again the government tried to clean up the housing problem, and many urban renewal projects were started. The lack of safe clean water was still a major problem all over the city, in particular the south-east, which was contaminated by the river Bièvre (a tributary of the Seine) whose waters were polluted by the Oberkampf factory at Jouy, to the south-west of Paris. A sixth city wall was built, not so much for defense against France's enemies, but as a customs barricade which the Fermiers Généraux of taxes controlled—ostensibly to protect the tax office from smuggling and fraud, but actually to squeeze every possible centime out of the farmers and traders.

Although still a great financial center, by the mid-18th century luxury handicrafts were the only real industry in Paris, and economic activity was limited to servicing and supplying its own population. The Bourse stock exchange had been created in 1724 and this was bolstered just over 50 years later by the creation of a central banking organization called the Caisse d'Escompte.

Since time immemorial the dead of Paris had been buried in city cemeteries around the churches, but the sheer numbers of the interred were causing problems of both space—there was no more—and pollution: the fumes given off by the dead in the Innocents graveyard were lethal to the living. So, starting in 1786 in a series of carefully respectful disinterments, blessed and overseen by the local parish priests, all the cemeteries in central Paris were cleared and the bones deposited in the huge underground catacombs of Place Denfert-Rochereau in the southern suburbs. Also, to assess the problem of city re-planning, the first detailed map of Paris was drawn up by Verniquet in 1787.

By Louis XVI's reign (1774–92) Paris was totally reliant on the countryside for food and supplies, and the free passage of farm produce, animals, grain, fruit, and vegetables depended on a settled and peaceful country. However the years 1787 and 1789 were blighted by particularly bad harvests in northern France. This led to food shortages and ultimately grain riots in Paris, and the start of almost ten years of continual riots and civil unrest caused by food shortages, crippling taxation, royal unpopularity, and general discontent.

Politicians argued to and fro over solutions until they finally agreed to hold the first National Assembly on June 17, 1789, and swore not to disband until they had drawn up a French constitution to limit royal autocracy and guarantee the liberty, equality, and fraternity of every Frenchman. Louis was greatly displeased and threatened to dissolve the assembly.

Civil discontent erupted one month later on July 14, 1789, when the Paris mob stormed their hated symbol of royal suppression—the Bastille. Revolution swept the whole of France, but the capital inevitably suffered more upheaval than anywhere else, although the other main centres of revolt—Le Havre, Nantes, Rennes, Lyon and Dijon—also endured huge disruption.

The first few months of Revolution witnessed numerous reforms which brought no halt to civil disorder or economic and political stability. One of the biggest changes was the nationalization of church lands and the outlawing of religion; when the Revolution started Paris contained 50 monasteries, 62 nunneries, 41 churches, 22 major chapels and 11 seminaries—rich targets which were rapidly sold off. Unfortunately, the church ran and administered the hospitals, which therefore disappeared with the clerics.

Seemingly everyone who could fled abroad or at least out of Paris to the country. Many aristocrats crossed the Channel to England. King Louis and Marie-Antoinette tried to escape but were caught and confined to the Tuileries. The French Republic was established on September 20, 1792, initially led by the moderate Girondins. Their policies proved too conciliatory for the firebrand Jacobins, led by Danton, Robespierre, and Marat, who took over the reins of power. The fearsome guillotine started work and no aristocrat was safe in Paris. The king, Louis XVI, was guillotined on January 21, 1793, in front of his cheering subjects in the Place de la Révolution (Place de la Concorde); Queen Marie-Antoinette went the same way a few months later.

In March 1793 the Committee of Public Safety held executive powers and mercilessly arrested and suppressed all suspected royalist sympathizers. In this period, known as "The Great Terror," many hapless unfortunates were sent to the constantly operating guillotine. The most notorious executioner, Henri Sanson, boasted a record 54 heads in 24 minutes.

The Revolution brought disruption to every aspect of French life—the provisioning of Paris (always precarious) crumbled into chaos causing enormous inflation on all foodstuffs leaving only bread as remotely affordable to the poor. Unemployment (all the luxury industry workers had lost their livelihood) led to depression and the inevitable riots. The properties of the aristocracy, nobility, church, foreigners, and royalist sympathizers were sold off—in total about an eighth of Parisian property—causing further economic decline. This economic and political chaos paved the way for the young Napoleon Bonaparte (1769–1821) to rise to power.

With the ending of the Terror the priests reappeared, only to find that many of their flock had forsaken religion forever. But after 1799 the church was able to reinstate sixty-two monasteries in Paris, and two years later most of the churches that had not fallen into terminal disrepair were returned, although some were given to the Protestants who could now worship openly (as could the Jews).

Paris became Napoleon's base but the city burghers were obstructive, so he took all power away from the city and created instead the Préfecture of Police in 1800 to control affairs. Furthermore, he wanted Paris to be the heart of his empire, so he ordered all remaining archives (many were destroyed during the Revolution) brought to Paris. The first population census of Paris after the troubles was taken in 1801 and reported 547,756 residents. This showed also that an urbanization program was necessary to regulate the spread of Paris. Napoleon ordered sixteen city cemeteries emptied of their contents. To feed Paris he reorganized the food distribution system and created specialized district markets.

Napoleon was determined to restore France to her international position of power and influence; as part of this plan he had himself crowned emperor by Pope Pius VII in Notre-Dame cathedral on May 18, 1804. Paris, too, had to

Above:
Pont Neuf

On the western tip of the Île de la Cité is the Pont Neuf, whose foundation stone
was laid in 1578. Opened in 1607, it is the oldest bridge in Paris and was the first
bridge over the Seine without the buildings so prevalent on medieval structures.

look the part, and Napoleon determined to make it the most beautiful city in
the world. Great public works were launched to embellish the city and provide
employment for the masses, all funded by the spoils of foreign conquests.

New bridges were built across the Seine, quays were rebuilt along the
riverside, and new sewers were created. Triumphal arches appeared at
Carrousel and Étoile, and the Grand Army Column was put up in the Place
Vendôme (it was destroyed during the Commune in 1871 on the orders of the
painter Courbet). Monuments were erected and new houses built pushing the
standard of living up everywhere except in overcrowded central Paris. The
population rose to 700,000.

But it was a time of war and Napoleon ran out of his earlier luck. On
March 31, 1814, after skirmishing on the heights of Montmartre, Paris sur-
rendered to the Grand Alliance. Napoleon was forced to abdicate at
Fontainebleau and was exiled first to the isle of Elba and, after his escape and
defeat at Waterloo, ultimately to St. Helena where he died. The Bourbon
monarchy was restored.

The Industrial Revolution took Paris unawares; as a non-manufacturing
city the changes were slow coming and created many workshops but few fac-
tories. In 1803 Le Pecq became the first steam railway line to enter Paris; by
1842 six lines converged on the city. Some street gas lighting appeared in 1808;
deemed a success it was increased to a wider area in 1819, and all over Paris
in 1829. This had the side effect of lighting the grand boulevards and starting
off real Parisian night life. The first public transport bus arrived in 1828.

Despite modern innovations, all but the wealthiest Parisians put up with dreadful living conditions. In 1833 a good half of the people living in the city came from the countryside seeking jobs, social advancement, and higher salaries. France was still predominantly rural with few large towns. The unskilled, uneducated, and unsophisticated rural poor flocked to Paris. The high density, rising rents, and poor sanitation only meant that their standard of living decreased. Crime and violence were rife; gangs terrorized the streets and prostitution was often the only way a woman could find the money to feed herself and her family. Between 1824 and 1847 a massive 80% of Parisians went to a pauper's grave. Such conditions encouraged the wealthier middle class to move away from the center to safer districts.

All these problems were aggravated by the continuing lack of water. The huge population created impossible sanitation problems and the sewers were constantly clogged and frequently overflowed. The inevitable happened in 1832 when a cholera epidemic—the first for 200 years—broke out and killed about 20,000 people, mostly from the slums, out of a total population of around 900,000. Between 1840 and 1844, to prevent the recurrence of disease, the contaminated river Bièvre was culveted underground and the noxious Montfaucon dump abandoned.

In 1840 Napoleon's body was brought to Paris in great state and installed under the Dôme des Invalides. As a tribute to him the Luxor obelisk was erected in the center of the Place de la Concorde. Yet still, despite the horrors of cholera, rural emigrants swelled Paris—the population doubled in 50 years to 1,053,897 in 1846. There was little work to be had as the large-scale building works had stopped, but some projects were undertaken. Three canals, including the Saint-Martin Canal, were dug, and a further 70 miles of sewers were dug. A number of the bigger boulevards were leveled and some pavements asphalted. The city walls were refurbished and fortified.

By 1848 Paris's social problems were again at breaking point; cholera returned that year with around 19,000 people dying, and rioting broke out, known as the "Three Glorious Days" (February 22, 23, 24). The main target was the monarchy. Louis-Philippe was duly overthrown, and elections brought in the Second Republic under Louis Napoleon (nephew of the great man) for whom almost 75% of the electorate voted. In December 1851 a *coup d'état* made him Emperor Napoleon III, and witnessed the start of the Second Empire.

Napoleon III realized he had to act to improve the dreadful squalor and lack of economic opportunity for his people. The growing railroad network came to his aid by bringing jobs and prosperity and France as a whole enjoyed

Right:

Notre-Dame

Built on the site of earlier Christian—and, probably, pagan—religious foundations, Notre-Dame and its statues have watched over Paris for nearly 800 years.

an economic upturn. The population started to grow again. In 1866 the population of Paris was 1,825,274 and by 1870 1,970,000.

The slums at the heart of Paris formed a lawless, impenetrable core, where all authority was ignored and revolt festered. This situation was intolerable — the emperor used the expropriation law of 1841 and 1850 against rental of insanitary housing to enforce his order that entire overpopulated districts and mazes of lanes be opened up and destroyed. To assist in planning the new city center he called on the services of such architects as Baron Haussmann. The land was accurately surveyed and the project divided into three phases expected to last 20 years. The project cost around 2,500,000,000 francs and was paid for by the city itself, state subsidies, various loans, and the sale of land.

The face of Paris was changed forever: the slums of La Cité were razed, and Haussmann organized the great boulevards into long, straight thoroughfares that converged on major intersections and architectural landmarks: the Rue de Rivoli was connected with the Rue St.-Antoine; the Boulevard Strasbourg and Boulevard St.-Michel were made into a north-south corridor, and the circle of grand boulevards was completed. Important roads had their cobbles replaced with asphalt, and the mileage of pavements was increased from 155 miles in 1842 to 683 miles in 1870. To improve the quality of life, Paris needed more open space where her citizens could breathe fresh air. The large green areas of the Bois de Boulogne, Bois de Vincennes, and Buttes-Chaumont became public parks in 1861. Town squares were also created, to bring a ten-fold increase of green space to 4,445 acres by 1870.

The water services were examined and reorganized by Belgrand. He introduced a two-tier system with spring water for drinking water and personal use, and river water for sanitation and street cleaning. By segregating water usage he was able to double Paris's water supply and bring water to the ground floor of half the houses in Paris. A new sewerage system was dug and completed by 1870.

While all this major redevelopment work progressed, in 1860 the city limit was expanded to swallow eighteen small surrounding towns that added a further 30–40,000 to the population. Paris by now had a reputation for being an exciting city with a high quality of life and plentiful opportunities for work, and as a consequence foreigners (especially Germans and Belgians) as well as Frenchmen flocked to the capital. This only revived the age-old problem of restrictive housing and high rents. The poor were driven out to the cheaper outskirts, especially to the new industrial zones that had sprung up in the wake of industrialization and the arrival of canals and railroads. Despite the efforts of the planners, the slums reappeared. All the rebuilding also meant that the wealthy and poor were completely separated. The rich lived in the new town houses built around the Champs-Élysées, Chaillot, and Parc Monceau. The middle class bourgeoisie filled and expanded the suburbs. All this meant that the twelve arrondissements of 1830s' Paris expanded to the twenty it has today.

For such a large, populous, and sprawling city, Paris had a vastly inadequate transport system. The first bus company had been created in 1854, and the riverboat omnibus service transporting passengers up and down the Seine in 1867. The new Belt Railway operated three trains an hour and had twenty-seven stations along its nineteen-mile length. The success of this commuter railway contributed to the growth of suburbs such as St.-Cloud and Versailles, and increased the value of suburban land and rents; it also provided much-needed employment for around 70,000 workers.

In 1870 France became embroiled in war with Prussia. Napoleon III was taken prisoner at Sedan and imprisoned in England, where he died three years later. The Second Empire was over and the Third Republic declared on September 4, 1870. The Prussians marched on Paris which they put under siege from September 20, 1870 until January 28, 1871.

Internally, Paris had a National Guard of 560,000 men, of which 110,000 were professional soldiers. Outside the walls 236,000 Germans spread out along a fifty-mile front and easily blockaded the city. They bombarded Paris into surrender—some 12,000 shells fell on the Left Bank killing nearly a hundred people, wounding 2,786, and destroying 1,400 houses. Food shortages became a problem after November. Unfortunately for Parisians, it was a particularly hard winter and food was in short supply; the animals in the zoo were slaughtered for food and no cat, dog, or rat was safe from the pot. However, the Parisians were able to manufacture a huge amount of ordnance: the Louvre was turned into an armament workshop; 400 cannon were made in four months at the Gare de Lyons, and gas balloons made at the Gare d'Orléans carried 2.5 million letters and 164 passengers out of Paris.

The French government forced Paris to surrender after convoking the National Assembly. The bombing stopped on January 28, 1871, and 20,000 German troops entered the city. When they marched away on March 3 they left behind an angry and disaffected population. (The very last German troops did not leave until September 1873.) The city had ground to a halt and all economic activity had ceased. The government stayed out of immediate danger in Versailles as they stopped the National Guard's pay. By March 18 Parisians had had enough; angered by their weak government and their humiliating concessions and heavy war indemnity to the Germans, the artisan eastern districts revolted and the Commune was proclaimed ten days later.

Paris was besieged again between May 22 and 28, this time by government troops; when they got into the city the retribution was brutal. The army infiltrated through the outlying gardens, over the rooftops and via the narrow streets. A bloody week followed of street fighting around hundreds of barricades. Snipers on the rooftops pinned down the fighters and the wide boulevards were lethally defended by canon fire. Much of the city center burned. The rebels were remorselessly driven back, until they reached Buttes-Chaumont and Père-Lachaise where they were butchered on March 29, 1871.

Above:

Jardin des Tuileries

The Tuileries gardens were opened during the reign of Louis XIV and became the first European park available to everyone—except servants, beggars, and soldiers.

The roll call was grim: 34,000 Communards were dead and almost 40,000 prisoners were interned at Versailles; about half of them were executed and a further 8,700 deported or detained. Many further victims were denounced by their neighbors and colleagues. Most of the victims were working class poor. The result was a total breakdown in the social order. Neighborhoods fragmented as the lower middle class and the proletariat—who had stood shoulder to shoulder at the barricades—were alienated from each other. Paris itself was badly damaged: the homes of the wealthy had been ransacked and entire streets were rubble; public buildings like the Hôtel de Ville were destroyed along with all the historic archives. Parts of the Tuileries palace were also badly damaged.

The Third Republic was established in 1871. Paris now had a population of 1,851,792 and was at saturation point again, with much of the influx coming from rural France where there were few opportunities for work. The government set about repairing the damage with a series of public works, including the basilica of Sacré-Coeur in Montmartre and the Palais du Trocadéro. However, by 1890 disillusioned peasants started returning to the countryside and new immigrants came to Paris. Persecutions in central Europe sent many Jews to Paris on their way to America; not all of them finished their journey, some 30,000 settling in Paris between 1881 and 1914.

The economic and social depression after the Commune lasted until 1886. The damaged Tuileries Palace was destroyed as an emblem of empire, and ruined buildings were still commonplace at the turn of the century. The city was still suffering the huge economic burden of Haussmann's regeneration, the politicians were venal and corrupt, and there was no overall ruling city authority. Despite all this the suburbs were still expanding, and a number of city streets were widened and the Avenue de l'Opéra completed.

The Paris Expositions took place in 1878, 1889, and 1900. The 1889 Exposition commemorated the centenary of the Revolution and left the Eiffel Tower as its legacy. With the excitement of the expositions and greater financial and social stability, the economy picked up, and both private and public funds went into building great public amenities such as schools, hospitals, and university facilities. The modernization of Paris was coming: electric lighting first arrived in 1878 at the Place de l'Opéra—fiercely blocked and obstructed by the gas companies; in 1881 the telephone arrived in Paris followed a few years later, in 1905, by the wireless station on the top of the Eiffel Tower.

The growth of Paris only accentuated the problem of the inadequacy of the public transport system. An erratic selection of trams, buses, trolley buses, cable cars, and riverboats on the Seine moved Parisians around the city. The French state wanted Paris to accept the underground connection of the major railway lines to facilitate passenger movement, but the city wanted its own independent underground system like those in London, New York, and Chicago. Paris decided its own fortune by building the Métro in defiance of state wishes; where it couldn't go underground it was built as an aerial railway. Furthermore the Métro was intentionally built with tunnels too narrow for conventional railway cars. The first line, Vincennes–Maillot, opened in July 1900 and was an immediate success with the public.

Housing was still a big headache. Building inspectors were appointed in 1879 to oversee safety standards. The poor were still being driven out of the center by high rents, even though in 1884 a reported 13% of families of six or more had more than one room. At last families started to decrease in size, but after the legalization of divorce in 1884 more single people needed accommodation. Comfort held a higher priority and was greatly increased as the elevator became more common. Records of building sanitation were started in 1893 and used to improve conditions.

Turn of the century Paris was a thriving and rapidly modernizing city. It had become the world center of culture, particularly for painters who flocked to live in Parisian garrets. Parisian night life—especially cabaret and music hall—was helped immeasurably by the arrival of artificial light, and then motion pictures arrived to take the public by storm. The first film was shown in Paris in 1895, and by 1911 the city had sixty-four movie theaters. Before World War I the city was booming, the only really bad setback was the great flood of Paris in 1910 when much of the city was under water.

The good life halted abruptly with the start of World War I. In spite of the threat of German troops reaching the city, Paris itself suffered little damage during the war, although at periods the sounds of battle could be heard. The city was bombed from long-range and was also the object of aerial bombardment with only localized affect. In 1914 rents were frozen at the lowest possible rate in an attempt to avoid inflation, and all construction ceased except in the very wealthiest areas. Spiraling costs aggravated by the shortage of workers and materials meant that buildings went unmaintained and unmodernized and there was general urban deterioration. Those speculators who did manage to build could do so without constraint.

On November 11, 1918, the Armistice was signed; on July 14, 1919, four to five million Parisians took to the streets to celebrate the victory. In a spirit of relief the city fortifications were destroyed (1919–24) and new boulevards laid out in their place. After the war and the heavy loss of young male lives, the population of France dropped, which in some measure alleviated the overcrowding problems.

Between 1911 and 1936 around 60,000 Parisians took the opportunity to move out of the city center, being replaced by a large foreign population, especially Jewish, political, and economic refugees from Russia and Poland. Despite the need to feed this population, the farms that still largely encircled Paris until the 20th century started to disappear as their agricultural land was overwhelmed by increasing industrialization. Those in the north and west disappeared first, where the railroads and canals made distribution of industrial goods easy, and Paris rapidly became encircled by industrial suburbs. Towns with a railway station grew ten times faster than those without.

The arrival of the motor car brought back an old problem to Paris—the sheer weight of traffic, as more and more people used private transport. Roads had to be widened across the city to accommodate their use. By now all French roads and rail lines converged on Paris; due to this and French political centralization, much of French industry was based around the capital. Jobs which were scarce in the rest of the country were easier to find around Paris, and rural immigration resumed on a huge scale.

The vast majority of newcomers lived in the suburbs, which grew by a massive 500%. Many who lived there commuted into Paris, even though public transport was slow and congested. To alleviate the situation the Métro was extended to facilitate the movement of workers and commuters, and also to provide much needed employment (it was finished in 1937). The suburbs were still growing haphazardly, without an overall authority to oversee and regulate the buildings. Accordingly many houses lacked any sanitary provision at all, and the owners and tenants had no money to improve conditions and amenities; in fact many people could not afford to even feed themselves.

The problem of the suburbs was recognized at high level by the Committee for the Organization and Expansion of the Paris Region in 1928, but French bureaucracy took until 1934 to decide on an urban plan and until 1939 to approve it. Meanwhile in the suburbs themselves, as their conditions worsened, discontent was brewing; political activists talked the people into first supporting socialism, then communism. Conversely, in Paris itself, the wealthy and middle classes moved to the right politically.

Jobs disappeared and businesses closed; the price of food and rents went up while supply went down. Ready as ever for civil action, the Paris mob took to the Place de la Concorde for a typically violent riot in January and February 1934, followed by numerous strikes and the creation of a ring of left wing suburbs known as the *ceinture rouge*.

Pre-World War II Paris was a sprawling conurbation of over six million people whose citizens lived in conditions six times the density of New York. The problems of inadequate housing and poor sanitation still plagued the city. There were not enough parks for Parisians as well as insufficient houses. Most attempts at a solution failed due to the lack of authority and maneuvering among the politicians.

War in Europe had erupted again in 1939 and, as the German troops marched on Paris in 1940, as many citizens as possible fled the city. The French government decided that the only way to avoid considerable damage was to concede the city without a fight. Consequently, when the Germans reached Paris on June 14, 1940, it was completely undefended and capitulated without a shot being fired. During the four years of occupation the city suffered little damage—by Hitler's express orders. The Germans were forced out of Paris August 19–26, 1944, leaving an intact but rapidly deteriorating housing stock and public facilities. As people returned to the city its problems became increasingly apparent: the Metro was in a state of disrepair, most of the city's buses had disappeared during the occupation; and despite the housing crisis there was no money to resume building and restoration—construction costs had risen by 40% since 1914.

Rents had been frozen in 1940 and tenants were protected from eviction; the population of Paris was as high as ever at 2,295,000 in 1941. Businesses were better off as they were less tightly regulated and some landlords were able to evict entire districts of their tenants. In September 1948 the law was changed to free the restrictions on landlords and construction resumed in a small way.

In October 1946 the Fourth Republic was declared, and for the first time women were given the vote. Problems were still manifest. As the economy improved, unchecked speculation saw the increase in the price of land and many private houses, gardens, and buildings were destroyed to make way for high density modern blocks. Pollution had worsened, caused by effluent from the industrial zones and the Parisians love of the personal motorcar. Roads were jammed with too many cars seeking too few parking spaces—emergency services, public transport, delivery trucks, and the cleaning operators could not do their jobs. The pollution doubled deaths from lung cancer, and chronic bronchitis increased by 20%.

The Fifth Republic was proclaimed in 1958 under the leadership of Charles de Gaulle, who was declared President for seven years. A new constitution was enacted and a new determination to deal with the persistent problems of the past was announced. Committees were set up and laws promulgated. The broad intention was to decentralize France and create a plan for the development of Paris which would resume abandoned projects such as the express Métro and radiating thoroughfares.

By 1960 Paris had a population of 3,035,000 and greater Paris (the Île-de-France region) a population of over eight million. Other cities around France now grew faster but enjoyed a lower population density. Between 1945 and 1960 over a million people arrived from the provinces, attracted as ever by the greater prospects of the capital: 60% of the population lived in the suburbs but only 40% worked there—the others commuted daily into the center.

Slowly but surely the face of Paris changed as it was fully modernized. The old Marais quarter was revamped and large scale public works were carried out. The Métro became state-of-the-art transport, the first overground RER (*Réseau Express Régional*) was opened in 1969; suburban rail lines were electrified and the railway stations modernized; the great road ring around Paris—the Périphérique—was constructed, and the river banks turned into roaring thoroughfares. Underground garages were constructed to get cars off the streets. The public utilities of water, gas and electricity were revised and streamlined, and new reservoirs and dams created on the Seine and Marne to supply much needed water to Paris. The university joined in by building new facilities. Amid great controversy the central market of Les Halles was demolished in the 1970s and moved further out to La Villette and Rungis.

In 1962 Algerian independence was declared and a new influx of immigrants flocked to Paris. By this time the capital had a diverse population of mixed ethnic origin and this was reflected in its restaurants, markets, and cultural life. Beside the immigrants, the inhabitants of central Paris were mostly the wealthy upper and middle classes; the working class and unemployed lived in the suburbs. Social unrest was prevalent but less focused until the student revolt over education policy in May 1968 brought the barricades to the streets of Paris again.

Expansion and building came to a halt in 1975 with the world-wide oil crisis; instead, Parisians started to conserve and develop their open spaces. A housing crisis arose again as too many people tried to squeeze into the city

Right:

The Eiffel Tower, Luxor Obelisk, and Statue

Three Parisian landmarks: the statue is one of eight huge sculptures in the Place de la Concorde, each of which represents one of the great towns of France.

which was made worse by restrictions on landlords. A change in policy was necessary before the construction boom of houses and offices started in 1988. In the last few years of the 20th century, Paris blossomed into a modern city with entire districts (especially in the east of Paris) remodeled. In Montparnasse, once a district of artists, writers, and poets, the old buildings have been demolished to make way for the new as part of a major urban renewal project which saw the building of the controversial Montparnasse Tower. A new opera house, the Bastille Opéra, was opened in 1990 on the Right Bank under the instigation of President François Mitterand. Another of his projects was the giant Arche de la Défense, completed in 1989. La Défense increasingly bristles with skyscrapers for international financial and business groups. Finally the Parc des Princes stadium was no longer the home of the French international rugby team which instead moved to the prestigious new Stade de France in St.-Denis and opened for France's victorious 1998 soccer world cup campaign. There are now thirty-one bridges across the Seine. In 1990 2,152,423 inhabitants lived in Paris and 9,152,423 in greater Paris making it one of the largest metropolitan areas in the world. As the city has sprouted offices, more people have moved out to the suburbs to commute into the city daily (about a million); another million commute in to the center to work.

Paris is still very much the heart and brains of France. It is still the fourth most important port in France—after Marseilles, Le Havre, and Dunkirk. The city is served by two international airports, Orly and Charles de Gaulle, and Le Bourget for internal domestic flights. Between 65 and 70% of French business and banking businesses have their headquarters in Paris and heavy industry still rings the outskirts. All this brings money into the city although the largest source of income is tourism as Paris attracts visitors from around the world. In 1976 Paris was granted municipal status in line with other French cities, which meant having a mayor again. The first was elected on March 25, 1977—a post often used as a steppingstone to the Presidency. The major is assisted by two prefects and a general council. The city is still divided into 20 arrondissements.

Paris means different things to different people—for some it is the ultimate city of romance, for others a great cradle of culture with its magnificent architecture and numerous art galleries, museums, theaters, and opera houses; for many people the very word alone means shopping and couture fashion. For the French themselves it is all these things and much much more—it is the center of French commercial, business, and political life, and the very heart of the nation.

Right:

Arc de Triomphe

The tomb of the Unknown Soldier lies below the Arc and contains one of the French dead after the Battle of Verdun. A flame of remembrance marks the spot.

Above and Right:
Arc de Triomphe
Started by Napoleon Bonaparte as "a monument dedicated to the Grand Army, grand, simple, and majestic, without anything borrowed from antique reminiscences," the Arc de Triomphe was designed by Chalgrin, built between 1806 and 1836 and is decorated with statues and reliefs on every side—some by Cortot, others by Étex, and La Marseillaise by Rude. There is an excellent museum inside, and splendid views towards La Défense and, down the Champs-Élysées, the Louvre.

Above:

Place de la Bastille

The new Opéra-Bastille in eastern Paris was designed by Carlos Ott; more impressive at night, during the day it is very austere. Inside it seats 2,700 and has a double stage. It is one of François Mitterand's architectural legacies to Paris, and opened on July 14, 1989, on the two hundreth anniversary of the French Revolution.

Right:

Bibliothèque Nationale

Since 1793 a copy of every publication printed in France has been lodged by law in this huge library — alongside the British Library it is one of the two largest in Europe.

Previous page:

Catacombs

Beneath the city streets Paris is riddled with catacombs; they have been used to hide resistance fighters, as ossuaries and burial grounds, and for quarrying stone.

Above:

Café de Flore

Café life in Paris is one of the main attractions of the city. They are the ideal place to sit in the sunshine and survey the passing street scene while enjoying a coffee, a beer or a light snack.

Right:

La Bourse

Built 1808–28 to architect Brongniart's design, with wings added 1902–07, the Bourse is Paris's stock exchange.

Above and Right:
Champs-Élysées
One of the most beautiful avenues in the world, the Avenue des Champs-Élysées runs along the same route as
the old road to Normandy, the rue du Faubourg-St.-Honoré, from the Place Charles de Gaulle Étoile,
where the Arc de Triomphe is situated, to the Place de la Concorde.
Noted for its restaurants and cafés, the avenue is dominated by the Arc at its western end.

Previous page:
Canal St.-Martin
The Canal St.-Martin runs underground for over a mile, passing underneath the Place de la Bastille
before re-surfacing in the Gare d'eau de l'Arsenal before joining the Seine.

Above and Right:
Champs-Élysées
Much of Paris is monumental, designed to impress, and the Champs-Élysées is no exception. Wide enough
to host the final leg of the annual Tour de France cycling race, it forms the perfect avenue for marching soldiers
— as was seen at the fall and, later, the liberation of Paris during World War II — and cheering crowds.
Few who were there will forget the size of the crowds, or their unabashed joy, following France's victory
in the 1998 soccer World Cup.

Above:
Place de l'Alma
The streets around the Place d'Alma contain the showrooms of many of the grand Parisian haut couture houses.

Right:
Place de la Concorde
The huge open square no longer rings to the crowds that watched Louis XVI, Marie-Antoinette, Robespierre and over 1,000 others lose their heads here to the guillotine. It is watched over today by the Luxor obelisk, erected in 1836. The hieroglyphs celebrate the pharaoh who had it made: Rameses II.

Above:

La Défense — La Grande Arche

Now the main business area of Paris, La Défense was so named after a monument commemorating the defense of Paris
against the Prussians in 1871. The most visible aspect, as seen from the Champs-Élysées, is the Grande Arche,
a 330ft high hollow cube adding a modern aspect to historic Paris.

Right:

La Défense — CNIT

The CNIT opened in 1958 as an exhibition hall, one of the early buildings in what has become an architectural showcase.

Above:

Tributes to Diana

The Flamme de la Liberté was covered with tributes to Diana, Princess of Wales after her death in August 1997
in the Pont d'Alma underpass.

Right:

Eiffel Tower

There's a wonderful vista from the gardens of the Trocadéro, across the Pont d'Iéna to the Eiffel Tower,
Champ-de-Mars and the 18th century École Militaire.

Above:

View from the Eiffel Tower

Paris spreads out like a map from the top of the Eiffel Tower—to the left and due north is the Arc de Triomphe
at the convergence of 12 great avenues.

Right:

Eiffel Tower

Built to last 20 years as a temporary exhibit for the Paris Exposition of 1889,
the Eiffel Tower has become synonymous with Paris.

Overleaf:

Fountains in the Jardins du Trocadéro

The ornamental lake of the Trocadéro, the renovated and rebuilt Palais de Chaillot, boasts marvelous fountains
including a battery of 20 jets which shoot almost horizontally towards the Seine.

Above and Right:
Grand Palais
Situated just off the Champs-Élysées next to the Pont-Alexandre III, the Grand Palais and the Petitit Palais—
its near neighbor across the Avenue Winston Churchill—were built for the Great Exhibition of 1900.
Criticized ever since for its architecture, the Grand Palais hides its metal framework behind
an impressive, colonnaded exterior. It sees regular use as an exhibition hall
and has hosted many major events—such as the 1925 International Exhibition of Decorative Arts
which saw Art Deco take the art world by storm.

Above and Previous Page:
Galeries Lafayette
Inside the Galeries Lafayette is a wonderful art-glass Art Nouveau dome supported by metal pillars.
It makes shopping even more of a joy!

Right:
Quai Malaquais
The Rive Gauche is noted for its secondhand booksellers — *bouquinistes* — whose stalls stretch from
the Quai St. Michel almost as far as the Musée d'Orsay.

Above:

Boulevard Haussmann

On Boulevard Haussmann stand Paris's best known department stores—Printemps and, illustrated here, Galeries
Lafayette, which boasts a wonderful central glass dome supported by pillars (see pages 60–61).

Right:

Hôtel de Ville

Paris's town hall was rebuilt to its original style between 1874 and 1882 after fire had destroyed it. In the past the huge
square in front—then known as the Place de Grève—was a place of execution.

Previous page:

Gare du Nord

The terminus for trains from northern France, the Channel ports and now the Eurostar link to Brussels and across to
England through the Channel Tunnel, the Gare du Nord's proud façade was designed by Jacques Hittorff.

Above and Right:
Les Invalides—Church of St. Louis

The Hôtel des Invalides was founded in 1671 by Louis XIV as a home for wounded and disabled soldiers.

The great church behind—St. Louis des Invalides, whose external dome is illustrated here—was begun in 1675

and finished in 1706. It is roofed with lead and adorned with huge gilded trophies.

There is an inner dome covered in frescoes that are illuminated indirectly.

Above:

Les Invalides — Tomb of Napoleon I

The ashes of Napoleon Bonaparte lie under the dome of Les Invalides, inside a sarcophagus
made from Finnish red porphyry designed by Louis-Joachim Visconti.

Right:

Les Invalides — Church of St. Louis

In 1989 the dome of Les Invalides was regilded by ten goldsmiths who used 555,000 gold leaves
which weighed a total of 27,830lb of pure gold.

Above:

Jardins du Palais Royal

Little remains of the original 17th century gardens; today the eight acres are lined with rows of trimmed lime trees
and the area is well known for its restaurants.

Right:

Les Halles

Seen here to the left of the new Les Halles shopping center is the church of Saint-Eustache which was long hidden
from view by the market buildings. The church was built between 1532 and 1637 and modeled on nearby
Notre-Dame. During the Revolution it became a Temple of Agriculture, and was damaged badly by fire
in 1840 after which it was restored.

Previous Page:

Jardins des Tuileries

The Tuileries gardens epitomize the French love of order and reason triumphing over nature. Originally set out by
André le Nôtre in 1666, the recently restored gardens remain largely true to his design.

Above and Right:
Les Halles

The modern shopping center on the site of the old market of Les Halles covers much of the site of the original 12 huge produce halls. The market was moved away from the city center to reduce the number of heavy trucks coming in to the heart of the city. The traders finally abandoned the halls in 1969 and vain attempts were made to preserve the buildings. Only one hall was rescued and re-erected in Nogent-sur-Marne.

Previous Page:
La Madeleine

Started in 1764 but only finished in 1842, this church was dedicated by Napoleon in 1806 to his Grand Army, now it hosts French celebrity showbiz funerals.

Above and Right:
Musée du Louvre — Pyramid

The Louvre was originally a fortress, then a royal residence; it was built, rebuilt, knocked down, and changed
over the centuries. The majority of the palace today houses the world famous museum,
which was renovated between 1981 and 1993 by architect I.M.Pei.
The most visible change sits in the narrowest part of the Place du Carrousel—the mystical glass pyramid
through which visitors enter the museum. Directly underneath, I.M.Pei created
a vast reception hall which radiates corridors out into the galleries.

Above:

Palais du Luxembourg

Home of the French Senate, the palace was built 1612–22 with gardens laid out by Marie de Medici, widow of Henri IV.

Right:

Métro

The wonderful Art Nouveau entrances of the Métro are the work of Henri Guimard (1867–1942) in 1900. City and state argued about the Métro—the city wanted an exclusive system within the city boundaries; the state wanted it to serve the suburbs. Finally, to prevent any future link-up, the tunnels were deliberately made too small for conventional trains and, in addition, traveled on the right, in the opposite direction to suburban trains.

Above:

Montmartre

Well-known for its many cafés and restaurants, Montmartre is a lively location for an evening meal.

Right:

Père-Lachaise Cemetery

Père-Lachaise cemetery was opened in 1804 and takes its name from from Louis XIV's confessor. It numbers many great French men and women among those buried there—Ingres, Corot, Hugo, Molière, Edith Piaf, Chopin— but is also famous to fans of the American band The Doors, whose singer, Jim Morrison, is buried here.

Previous page:

Mémorial des Martyrs Français de la Déportation

At the east end of the Square de l'Île de France, on the eastern tip of the Île de la Cité, is a memorial to the 200,000 French men and women deported to German concentration camps during World War II.

Above:
Moulin Rouge

On the way to Montmartre, on the Boulevard de Clichy, is the Moulin Rouge—the Red Windmill. As a nightclub it
was synonymous with glamorous but naughty night-life; it has now become a movie theater.

Right and Previous page:
Musée d'Orsay

Once the Gare d'Orsay, it was built by the Orléans Railway Company as the Paris terminus
for trains to Nantes, Bordeaux, and Toulouse. When the network stopped in 1939 the building was used for
a variety of purposes but was eventually deemed unwieldy and threatened with demolition in 1961.
After the loss of Les Halles, Parisians were more aware of their architectural heritage and
fought to save the building. At the last moment the station was saved for the nation
and turned into a museum specializing in 19th and 20th century art.

Above and Right:
Notre-Dame de Paris Cathedral
Built on the site of earlier Christian—and, probably, pagan—religious foundations, Notre-Dame has watched over
Paris for nearly 800 years. The west front (*above*) is dominated by two towers, built between 1225 and 1250, from
which a stunning view of Paris can be enjoyed, and the great (59ft x 43ft) 13th century rose window.
The view of the cathedral from the Île St.-Louis (right) shows off the flying buttresses
that support the *Chevet* (the apse and ambulatory).

Above:

Notre-Dame de Paris Cathedral

The gargoyles—*chimières*—include fantastical carvings of birds, beasts, and devils. They were designed by
Viollet-le-Duc. Such grotesque demons were a popular feature of Gothic churches.

Right:

Bateau Mouche

A river trip on the Seine by Bateau Mouche is one of the best ways to see Notre-Dame, the Île de la Cité,
and the Île St.-Louis, as well as the other wonderful riverside buildings.

Overleaf:

Palais de Chaillot

Seen over the fountains of the Trocadéro, the Palais was built for the Paris Exhibition of 1937.
It now houses four museums and the TNP, the National Theater of Paris.

Above:

Opéra

A wonderful example of Belle Époque architecture at its best, with exuberant decorative motifs and statues —
amazingly, the Opéra was built within 75 frantic days. The façade has busts, masks, and sculptures of famous com-
posers and librettists. On the top of the dome over the auditorium is the gilt statue of Apollo Raising his Lyre by
Millet.

Right:

Palais de Justice

On the western side of the Île de la Cité are the principal law courts of Paris. The original medieval
Palais was damaged badly during the Revolution and rebuilt.

Overleaf:

Place des Vosges

Situated in the Marais, this is one of the most beautiful and historically interesting squares in Paris.

Above:

Place du Tertre

Montmartre's favorite tourist spot was created in 1635 on land given by Montmartre Abbey.

Right:

Place Vendôme

The Vendôme Column was made 1806–10 and has a spiral of 425 bas-relief plaques made from the metal of 250 Austrian and Russian bronze cannon. The plaques show the glorious triumphs of Napoleon's Austerlitz campaign. The (replacement) statue of Napoleon was almost destroyed in 1871 by a group of Communards.

Above and Right:
Palais Royal
Built by the great Cardinal Richelieu and given to the monarchy on his death in 1642, the Palais Royal became known
in his time for its associations with the stage (under Richelieu there were two theaters) and Molière put on the first
production of *School for Husbands* there in 1661. The calm exterior and pleasant gardens of the Palais Royal
hide a less salubrious past. Given by Louis XIV to his brother Philippe d'Orléans, it would remain in
the family's hands until 1848; during which time it became notorious for
prostitution and gambling. The Palais was reconstructed
between 1764 and 1770 after destruction by fire.

Previous page:
Place du Tertre
Ringed with bars and restaurants, this popular tourist spot is filled with artists selling their works and who
(for a price) will paint, sketch or do a caricature for you.

Above:

Parc de Monceau

These are the remains of an 18th century private park laid out in the then fashionable *Anglo-chinois* style. It contains a
grotto, follies, and an Italianate bridge, as well as abundant bird life attracted by the plants and trees.

Right:

Petit Palais

Built alongside the Grand Palais for the 1900 Exhibition, since 1902 the Petit Palais has housed municipal art
collections of works donated to the city by private collectors; the building is also used for temporary exhibitions.

Above and Right:
Georges Pompidou Center

An international architectural competition was held to find the best design for the proposed new cultural center
planned by President Pompidou. It was won by Richard Rogers and Renzo Piano with a controversial design.
The building was the first to have all its functional elements on the exterior instead of hidden inside the
walls. The Georges Pompidou Center opened in 1977, three years after Pompidou died.
It contains the National Museum of Modern Art, the Public Information Library, the Industrial Design Center,
and the Institute of Acoustic and Musical Research. In the late 1990s the Pompidou Center
underwent extensive remodeling and repairs under the direction of Renzo Piano.

Above and Right:
Pont Alexandre III
Built in 1900, the bridge is named after the Russian Tsar with whom France established an alliance in 1893.
The lamps are copied from examples found on Trinity Bridge in St. Petersburg. Expressly designed by architect
d'Albry not to impede the view of Les Invalides, the foundation stone was laid by Tsar Nicholas II
on October 7, 1896, and opened in 1900 at the same time as the Universal Exhibition.
It was constructed as the link over the Seine for a new triumphal avenue
between the Élysée Palace and the Hôtel des Invalides.

Above:

Pont Alexandre III

The exuberant style of decoration was specifically concocted to combine conventional stonework with the latest metallurgic technology that France wanted to show off to the world at the Universal Exhibition of 1900.

Right:

Pont au Change

The first bridge was built in 1304 during the reign of Philippe IV the Fair and was the center for moneylenders and financiers. It was rebuilt in stone in 1621, demolished in 1860, and rebuilt to carry the boulevard de Sébastopol.

Above:

Rue Mouffetard

Rue Mouffetard runs downhill from Place de la Contrescape to the church of the saint
who gave his name to this area—St. Médard.

Right:

Printemps

One of the biggest department stores in Paris, most of the main building dates from 1881 and is
Art Nouveau in style. The second building was rebuilt after a fire in 1921.

Above and Right:
Sacré-Cœur
Construction of the great white basilica of Sacré-Cœur was started in 1877: it would take forty years to finish.

Luckily, for those who decide against the steep walk up, there is a railway at the side.

When lit up at night, Sacré-Cœur is visible all over Paris.

Above:

Sacré-Cœur

The basilica has a number of impressive monuments and statues.

Right:

Sainte Chapelle

This Gothic masterpiece was built in 1243–48 by St. Louis to house his collection of relics—including a piece of the True Cross and the Crown of Thorns. The chapel, noted for its splendid stained glass windows, was badly damaged during the Revolution and heavily but beautifully restored in the 19th century.

Above:

St.-Germain-des-Pres

The oldest church in Paris, St.-Germain-des-Pres is noted for its Romanesque architecture.

Right:

Statue of Liberty

On the southern tip of the Allée des Cygnes, just downriver from the Eiffel Tower and alongside the
Pont de Grenelle, is a miniature bronze replica of Bartholdi's famous statue.

Previous page:

St. Eustache

Consecrated in 1637, this is essentially a Renaissance building built on a medieval plan. In 1795 it became the
Temple of Agriculture for the duration of the Revolution. Molière was baptized here in 1622 and
Minister Colbert and Admiral de Tourville are among those buried here.

Above:

Clignancourt Market

Once a flea market, today's massive mixture of clothes, antiques, and bric-à-brac rivals any in Europe. This view of permanent covered stores does not prepare the visitor for the crowds spilling out over the open areas of the market!

Right:

Tour St.-Jacques

The only remains of the church of St. Jacques-la-Boucherie which was demolished in 1797, the tower itself dates from 1508–22. It was used as a shot tower after 1836 until 1858.

INDEX